MJF BOOKS | NEW YORK

THE
UNDISCOVERED COUNTRY

PHOTOGRAPHY BY GARY HART

EDITED BY JACQUELINE VARY

Published by MJF Books
Fine Communications
322 Eighth Avenue
New York, NY 10001

The Undiscovered Country

LC Control Number: 2009925280
ISBN-13: 978-1-56731-967-5
ISBN-10: 1-56731-967-X

Printed in Singapore.

DESIGNED BY LISA CHOVNICK

MJF Books and the MJF colophon are trademarks of Fine Creative Media, Inc.

TWP   10   9   8   7   6   5   4   3   2   1

CONTENTS

THE
UNDISCOVERED
COUNTRY

The Undiscovered Country

Man has explored all countries and all lands,
    And made his own the secrets of each clime.
Now, ere the world has fully reached its prime,
The oval earth lies compassed with steel bands,
The seas are slaves to ships that touch all strands,
    And even the haughty elements sublime
    And bold, yield him their secrets for all time,
And speed like lackeys forth at his commands.

Still, though he search from shore to distant shore,
    And no strange realms, no unlocated plains
Are left for his attainment and control,
Yet is there one more kingdom to explore.
    Go, know thyself, O man! there yet remains
The undiscovered country of thy soul!

—ELLA WHEELER WILCOX

Dawn

Ecstatic bird songs pound
the hollow vastness of the sky
with metallic clinkings—
beating color up into it
at a far edge,—beating it, beating it
with rising, triumphant ardor,—
stirring it into warmth,
quickening in it a spreading change,—
bursting wildly against it as
dividing the horizon, a heavy sun
lifts himself—is lifted—
bit by bit above the edge
of things,—runs free at last
out into the open—! lumbering
glorified in full release upward—

                songs cease.

—WILLIAM CARLOS WILLIAMS

A Psalm of Life

What the heart of the young man said to the psalmist.

Tell me not, in mournful numbers,
    "Life is but an empty dream!"
For the soul is dead that slumbers,
    And things are not what they seem.

Life is real! Life is earnest!
    And the grave is not its goal;
"Dust thou art, to dust returnest,"
    Was not spoken of the soul.

Not enjoyment, and not sorrow,
    Is our destined end or way;
But to act, that each to-morrow
    Find us farther than to-day.

Art is long, and Time is fleeting,
    And our hearts, though stout and brave,
Still, like muffled drums, are beating
    Funeral marches to the grave.

In the world's broad field of battle,
    In the bivouac of Life,

Be not like dumb, driven cattle!
    Be a hero in the strife!

Trust no Future, howe'er pleasant!
    Let the dead Past bury its dead!
Act,—act in the living Present!
    Heart within, and God o'erhead!

Lives of great men all remind us
    We can make our lives sublime,
And, departing, leave behind us
    Footprints on the sands of time;

Footprints, that perhaps another,
    Sailing o'er life's solemn main,
A forlorn and shipwrecked brother,
    Seeing, shall take heart again.

Let us, then, be up and doing,
    With a heart for any fate;
Still achieving, still pursuing,
    Learn to labor and to wait.

— HENRY WADSWORTH LONGFELLOW

My Prayer

Great God, I ask thee for no meaner pelf
Than that I may not disappoint myself;
That in my action I may soar as high
As I can now discern with this clear eye.

And next in value, which thy kindness lends,
That I may greatly disappoint my friends,
Howe'er they think or hope that it may be,
They may not dream how thou'st distinguished me.

That my weak hand may equal my firm faith,
And my life practise more than my tongue saith;
That my low conduct may not show,
Nor my relenting lines,
That I thy purpose did not know,
Or overrated thy designs.

— HENRY DAVID THOREAU

From

Song of the Open Road

Afoot and light-hearted I take to the open road,

Healthy, free, the world before me,

The long brown path before me leading wherever I choose.

Henceforth I ask not good-fortune, I myself am good-fortune,

Henceforth I whimper no more, postpone no more, need nothing,

Done with indoor complaints, libraries, querulous criticisms,

Strong and content I travel the open road.

The earth, that is sufficient,

I do not want the constellations any nearer,

I know they are very well where they are,

I know they suffice for those who belong to them.

(Still here I carry my old delicious burdens,

I carry them, men and women, I carry them with me wherever I go,

I swear it is impossible for me to get rid of them

I am fill'd with them, and I will fill them in return.)

— WALT WHITMAN

I Will Be Worthy of It

I may not reach the heights I seek,
    My untried strength may fail me;
Or, half-way up the mountain peak
    Fierce tempests may assail me.
But though that place I never gain,
Herein lies comfort for my pain—
    I will be worthy of it.

I may not triumph in success,
    Despite my earnest labor;
I may not grasp results that bless
    The efforts of my neighbor.
But though my goal I never see
This thought shall always dwell with me—
    I will be worthy of it.

The golden glory of Love's light
    May never fall on my way;
My path may always lead through night,
    Like some deserted by-way.
But though life's dearest joy I miss
There lies a nameless strength in this—
    I will be worthy of it.

—ELLA WHEELER WILCOX

23

The Apology

Think me not unkind and rude,
That I walk alone in grove and glen;
I go to the god of the wood
To fetch his word to men.

Tax not my sloth that I
Fold my arms beside the brook;
Each cloud that floated in the sky
Writes a letter in my book.

Chide me not, laborious band,
For the idle flowers I brought;
Every aster in my hand
Goes home loaded with a thought.

There was never mystery
But 'tis figured in the flowers;
Was never secret history
But birds tell it in the bowers.
One harvest from thy field
Homeward brought the oxen strong;
A second crop thine acres yield,
Which I gather in a song.

— RALPH WALDO EMERSON

From

Miracles

Why, who makes much of a miracle?

As to me I know of nothing else but miracles,

Whether I walk the streets of Manhattan,

Or dart my sight over the roofs of houses toward the sky,

Or wade with naked feet along the beach just in the edge of the water,

Or stand under trees in the woods,

Or talk by day with any one I love, or sleep in the bed at night with any one I love,

Or sit at table at dinner with the rest,

Or look at strangers opposite me riding in the car,

Or watch honey-bees busy around the hive of a summer forenoon,

Or animals feeding in the fields,

Or birds, or the wonderfulness of insects in the air,

Or the wonderfulness of the sundown, or of stars shining so quiet and bright,

Or the exquisite delicate thin curve of the new moon in spring;

These with the rest, one and all, are to me miracles,

The whole referring, yet each distinct and in its place.

— WALT WHITMAN

Revelation

We make ourselves a place apart
    Behind light words that tease and flout,
But oh, the agitated heart
    Till someone find us really out.

'Tis pity if the case require
    (Or so we say) that in the end
We speak the literal to inspire
    The understanding of a friend.

But so with all, from babes that play
    At hide-and-seek to God afar,
So all who hide well away
    Must speak and tell us where they are.

— ROBERT FROST

From

Songs of a Girl

I am not afraid of my own heart.
I am not afraid of what may be in the places where
    the shadows are piled.
I am not afraid—see, I walk straight in
And look everywhere.
I am not afraid—ah, what was that?

It is a dangerous place in which to walk—a heart.
Especially one's own.

.   .   .   .

There are three of us; the little girl I used to be, the
    girl I am, and the woman I am going to be. We
    take counsel together concerning what colors we
    shall weave into the dram that we are making.

Sometimes they say, she is day-dreaming,
    they do not know that we are taking counsel together,
    the little girl, and the girl I am, and the woman
    that I am going to be.
There are many things that they do not know.

—MARY CAROLYN DAVIES

The Door

The littlest door, the inner door,
    I swing it wide.
Now in my heart there is no more
    To hide.

The farthest door—the latch at last
    Is lifted; see
I kept the little fortress fast.
    —Be good to me.

—MARY CAROLYN DAVIES

Afternoon on a Hill

I will be the gladdest thing
    Under the sun!
I will touch a hundred flowers
    And not pick one.

I will look at cliffs and clouds
    With quiet eyes,
Watch the wind bow down the grass,
    And the grass rise.

And when lights begin to show
    Up from the town,
I will mark which must be mine,
    And then start down!

— EDNA ST. VINCENT MILLAY

I Know Not Why

I lift mine eyes against the sky,
The clouds are weeping, so am I;
I lift mine eyes again on high,
The sun is smiling, so am I.
Why do I smile? Why do I weep?
I do not know; it lies too deep.

I hear the winds of autumn sigh,
They break my heart, they make me cry;
I hear the birds of lovely spring,
My hopes revive, I help them sing.
Why do I sing? Why do I cry?
It lies so deep, I know not why.

— MORRIS ROSENFELD

Petals

Life is a stream

On which we strew

Petal by petal the flower of our heart;

The end lost in dream,

They float past our view,

We only watch their glad, early start.

Freighted with hope,

Crimsoned with joy,

We scatter the leaves of our opening rose;

Their widening scope,

Their distant employ,

We never shall know. And the stream as it flows

Sweeps them away,

Each one is gone

Ever beyond into infinite ways.

We alone stay

While years hurry on,

The flower fared forth, though its fragrance still stays.

— AMY LOWELL

Paradox

I went out to the woods to-day
    To hide away from you,
From you a thousand miles away —
    But you came, too.

And yet the old dull thought would stay,
    And all my heart benumb —
If you were but a mile away
    You would not come.

—JESSIE B. RITTENHOUSE

Experience

This morning I looked at the map of the day
And said to myself, "This is the way! This is the way I will go;
Thus shall I range on the roads of achievement,
The way is so clear — it shall all be a joy on the lines marked out."
And then as I went came a place that was strange, —
'Twas a place not down on the map!
And I stumbled and fell and lay in the weeds,
And looked on the day with rue.

I am learning a little — never to be sure —
To be positive only with what is past,
And to peer sometimes at the things to come
As a wanderer treading the night
When the mazy stars neither point nor beckon,
And of all the roads, no road is sure.

I see those men with maps and talk
Who tell how to go and where and why;
I hear with my ears the words of their months,
As they finger with ease the marks on the maps;
And only as one looks robust, lonely, and querulous,
As if he had gone to a country far
And made for himself a map,
Do I cry to him, "I would see your map!
I would heed that map you have!"

— CARL SANDBURG

Each Life Converges to Some Centre

Each life converges to some centre
Expressed or still;
Exists in every human nature
A goal,

Admitted scarcely to itself, it may be,
Too fair
For credibility's temerity
To dare.

Adored with caution, as a brittle heaven,
To reach
Were hopeless as the rainbow's raiment
To touch,

Yet persevered toward, surer for the distance;
How high
Unto the saints' slow diligence
The sky!

Ungained, it may be, by a life's low venture,
But then,
Eternity enables the endeavoring
Again.

— EMILY DICKINSON

Leaving Markers

By the time you learn the directions
the signs have changed.
It is a question of trust not
of what they have promised.
You look away, astonished.

Leave markers you think.
For the way back.
So, you cut lines into trees,
pile stones at the bases of their trunks.
You watch the angle of the sun
and continue walking.

You look down, liking
the way your feet move out,
one foot in front of the other,
swinging your arms,
breathing deeply.

On your right, the sun rolls with you
over the rim of dark trees
then seems to rise up again.

Is this the right way?
You look for signs of the town.
The road dips, darkens.
The sky breaks into the branches.
Your breathing.
The crunch of your shoes.

You follow the widening road
through its curve passing a hemlock,
a pile of stones in front.
You lie down, placing your head on the stones,
fitting your body into the bumpy ground,
to discover how comfortable
hardness can be.
To mark the way forward
simply by taking it.

Will others follow?
Or will they mark some other way to go
and learn by going?

— MARLENE ROSEN FINE

Nothing But Leaves

Nothing but leaves; the spirit grieves
    Over a wasted life;
Sin committed while conscience slept,
Promises made, but never kept,
    Hatred, battle, and strife;
      Nothing but leaves!

Nothing but leaves; no garnered sheaves
    Of life's fair, ripened grain;
Words, idle words, for earnest deeds;
We sow our seeds,—lo! tares and weeds:
    We reap, with toil and pain,
      Nothing but leaves!

Nothing but leaves; memory weaves
    No veil to screen the past:
As we retrace our weary way,
Counting each lost and misspent day,
    We find, sadly, at last,
      Nothing but leaves!

And shall we meet the Master so,
    Bearing our withered leaves?
The Saviour looks for perfect fruit,
We stand before him, humbled, mute;
    Waiting the words he breathes,—
      "Nothing but leaves?"

—LUCY E. AKERMAN

All Lovely Things Will Have an Ending

All lovely things will have an ending,
All lovely things will fade and die,
And youth, that's now so bravely spending,
Will beg a penny by and by.

Fine ladies all are soon forgotten,
And goldenrod is dust when dead,
The sweetest flesh and flowers are rotten
And cobwebs tent the brightest head.

Come back, true love! Sweet youth, return!—
But time goes on, and will, unheeding,
Though hands will reach, and eyes will yearn,
And the wild days set true hearts bleeding.

Come back, true love! Sweet youth, remain!—
But goldenrod and daisies wither,
And over them blows autumn rain,
They pass, they pass, and know not whither.

—CONRAD AIKEN

The Rainy Day

The day is cold, and dark, and dreary;
It rains, and the wind is never weary;
The vine still clings to the mouldering wall,
But at every gust the dead leaves fall,
And the day is dark and dreary.

My life is cold, and dark, and dreary;
It rains, and the wind is never weary;
My thoughts still cling to the mouldering Past,
But the hopes of youth fall thick in the blast,
And the days are dark and dreary.

Be still, sad heart! and cease repining;
Behind the clouds is the sun still shining;
Thy fate is the common fate of all,
Into each life some rain must fall,
Some days must be dark and dreary.

—HENRY WADSWORTH LONGFELLOW

The Snow Storm

Announced by all the trumpets of the sky,
Arrives the snow, and, driving o'er the fields,
Seems nowhere to alight: the whited air
Hides hills and woods, the river, and the heaven,
And veils the farm-house at the garden's end.
The sled and traveller stopped, the courier's feet
Delayed, all friends shut out, the house-mates sit
Around the radiant fireplace, enclosed
In a tumultuous privacy of storm.

Come see the northwind's masonry.
Out of an unseen quarry evermore
Furnished with tile, the fierce artificer
Curves his white bastions with projected roof
Round every windward stake, or tree, or door.

Speeding, the myriad-handed, his wild work
So fanciful, so savage, naught cares he
For number or proportion. Mockingly,
On coop or kennel he hangs Parian wreaths;
A swan-like form invests the hidden thorn;
Fills up the farmer's lane from wall to wall,
Maugre the farmer's sighs; and at the gate,
A tapering turret overtops the work.
And when his hours are numbered, and the world
Is all his own, retiring, as he were not,
Leaves, when the sun appears, astonished Art
To mimic in slow structures, stone by stone,
Built in an age, the mad wind's night-work,
The frolic architecture of snow.

— RALPH WALDO EMERSON

The Snow Man

One must have a mind of winter
To regard the frost and the boughs
Of the pine-trees crusted with snow;

And have been cold a long time
To behold the junipers shagged with ice,
The spruces rough in the distant glitter

Of the January sun; and not to think
Of any misery in the sound of the wind,
In the sound of a few leaves,

Which is the sound of the land
Full of the same wind
That is blowing in the same bare place

For the listener, who listens in the snow,
And, nothing himself, beholds
Nothing that is not there and the nothing that is.

— WALLACE STEVENS

There's a Certain Slant of Light

There's a certain slant of light,
On winter afternoons,
That oppresses, like the weight
Of cathedral tunes.

Heavenly Hurt, it gives us;
We can find no scar,
But internal difference
Where the meanings, are.

None may teach it anything,
'Tis the seal despair, —
An imperial affliction
Sent us of the air.

When it comes, the landscape listens,
Shadows hold their breath;
When it goes, 'tis like the distance
On the look of death.

— EMILY DICKINSON

Loss and Gain

When I compare
What I have lost with what I have gained,
What I have missed with what attained,
   Little room do I find for pride.

I am aware
How many days have been idly spent;
How like an arrow the good intent
   Has fallen short or been turned aside.

But who shall dare
To measure loss and gain in this wise?
Defeat may be victory in disguise;
   The lowest ebb is the turn of the tide.

—Henry Wadsworth Longfellow

From

Song of Myself

The spotted hawk swoops by and accuses me, he complains of my gab and my loitering.

I too am not a bit tamed, I too am untranslatable,
I sound my barbaric yawp over the roofs of the world.

The last scud of day holds back for me,
It flings my likeness after the rest and true as any on the shadow'd wilds,
It coaxes me to the vapor and the dusk.

I depart as air, I shake my white locks at the runaway sun,
I effuse my flesh in eddies, and drift it in lacy jags.

I bequeath myself to the dirt to grow from the grass I love,
If you want me again look for me under your boot-soles.

You will hardly know who I am or what I mean,
But I shall be good health to you nevertheless,
And filter and fibre your blood.

Failing to fetch me at first keep encouraged,
Missing me one place search another,
I stop somewhere waiting for you.

— WALT WHITMAN

O Me! O Life!

O me! O life! of the questions of these recurring,

Of the endless trains of the faithless, of cities fill'd with the foolish,

Of myself forever reproaching myself, (for who more foolish than I, and who more faithless?)

Of eyes that vainly crave the light, of the objects mean, of the struggle ever renew'd,

Of the poor results of all, of the plodding and sordid crowds I see around me,

Of the empty and useless years of the rest, with the rest me intertwined,

The question, O me! so sad, recurring—What good amid these, O me, O life?

Answer

That you are here—that life exists and identity,

That the powerful play goes on, and you may contribute a verse.

— WALT WHITMAN

The Road Not Taken

Two roads diverged in a yellow wood,
And sorry I could not travel both
And be one traveler, long I stood
And looked down one as far as I could
To where it bent in the undergrowth;

Then took the other, as just as fair,
And having perhaps the better claim
Because it was grassy and wanted wear,
Though as for that the passing there
Had worn them really about the same,

And both that morning equally lay
In leaves no step had trodden black.
Oh, I marked the first for another day!
Yet knowing how way leads on to way
I doubted if I should ever come back.

I shall be telling this with a sigh
Somewhere ages and ages hence:
Two roads diverged in a wood, and I,
I took the one less traveled by,
And that has made all the difference.

— ROBERT FROST

From

Six Significant Landscapes

When my dream was near the moon,

The white folds of its gown

Filled with yellow light.

The soles of its feet

Grew red.

Its hair filled

With certain blue crystallizations

From stars,

Not far off.

.   .   .   .

Rationalists, wearing square hats,

Think, in square rooms,

Looking at the floor,

Looking at the ceiling.

They confine themselves

To right-angled triangles.

If they tried rhomboids,

Cones, waving lines, ellipses—

As, for example, the ellipse of the half-moon—

Rationalists would wear sombreros.

—WALLACE STEVENS

Madman's Song

Better to see your cheek grown hollow,

Better to see your temple worn,

Than to forget to follow, follow,

After the sound of a silver horn.

Better to bind your brow with willow

And follow, follow until you die,

Than to sleep with your head on a golden pillow,

Nor lift it up when the hunt goes by.

Better to see your cheek grown sallow

And your hair grown gray, so soon, so soon,

Than to forget to hallo, hallo,

After the milk-white hounds of the moon.

—ELINOR WYLIE

Crepuscule

I will wade out

                  till my thighs are steeped in burn-

ing flowers

I will take the sun in my mouth

and leap into the ripe air

                    Alive

                        with closed eyes

to dash against darkness

                        in the sleeping curves of my

body

Shall enter fingers of smooth mastery

with chasteness of sea-girls

                        Will I complete the mystery

of my flesh

I will rise

              After a thousand years

lipping

flowers

          And set my teeth in the silver of the moon

—E.E. CUMMINGS

When I Heard the Learn'd Astronomer

When I heard the learn'd astronomer,

When the proofs, the figures, were ranged in columns before me,

When I was shown the charts and diagrams, to add, divide and measure them,

When I sitting heard the astronomer where he lectured with much applause in the lecture-room,

How soon unaccountable I became tired and sick,

Till rising and gliding out I wander'd off by myself,

In the mystical moist night-air, and from time to time,

Look'd up in perfect silence at the stars.

— WALT WHITMAN

Morning Song

A diamond of a morning
    Waked me an hour too soon;
Dawn had taken in the stars
    And left the faint white moon.

O white moon, you are lonely,
    It is the same with me,
But we have the world to roam over,
    Only the lonely are free.

— SARA TEASDALE

The Lamp of Life

Always we are following a light,
    Always the light recedes; with groping hands
    We stretch toward this glory, while the lands
We journey through are hidden from our sight
Dim and mysterious, folded deep in night,
    We care not, all our utmost need demands
    Is but the light, the light! So still it stands
Surely our own if we exert our might.
Fool! Never can'st thou grasp this fleeting gleam,
    Its glowing flame would die if it were caught,
Its value is that it doth always seem
    But just a little farther on. Distraught,
    But lighted ever onward, we are brought
Upon our way unknowing, in a dream.

—AMY LOWELL

A Dream within a Dream

Take this kiss upon the brow!
And, in parting from you now,
Thus much let me avow:
You are not wrong, who deem
That my days have been a dream;
Yet if hope has flown away
In a night, or in a day,
In a vision, or in none,
Is it therefore the less gone?
All that we see or seem
Is but a dream within a dream.

I stand amid the roar
Of a surf-tormented shore,
And I hold within my hand
Grains of the golden sand—
How few! yet how they creep
Through my fingers to the deep,
While I weep, while I weep!
O God! can I not grasp
Them with a tighter clasp?
O God! can I not save
One from the pitiless wave?
Is all that we see or seem
But a dream within a dream?

—EDGAR ALLAN POE

The Tide Rises, the Tide Falls

The tide rises, the tide falls,
The twilight darkens, the curlew calls;
Along the sea-sands damp and brown
The traveller hastens toward the town,
    And the tide rises, the tide falls.

Darkness settles on roofs and walls,
But the sea, the sea in darkness calls;
The little waves, with their soft, white hands,
Efface the footprints in the sands,
    And the tide rises, the tide falls.

The morning breaks; the steeds in their stalls
Stamp and neigh, as the hostler calls;
The day returns, but nevermore
Returns the traveller to the shore.
    And the tide rises, the tide falls.

—Henry Wadsworth Longfellow

About the Photographer

Gary Hart is a photographer and writer living in Sacramento, California. When he's not photographing nature's splendor, Gary sells prints of his images and shares his vision via photo workshops and private photo tours in some of America's most beautiful landscapes. To learn more, visit Gary's website, www.eloquentimages.com.

About the Editor

Jacqueline Vary has a master's degree in American studies and works as a freelance writer and editor. She lives in northern New Jersey with her loving husband, their two sons, and a Tibetan Mastiff named Oliver Wendell Holmes, aka Ollie.

Hello, Beautiful!

Colorful Animals

WORLD
BOOK

www.worldbook.com

World Book, Inc.
180 North LaSalle Street, Suite 900
Chicago, Illinois 60601
USA

For information about other World Book
publications, visit our website at
www.worldbook.com or call
1-800-WORLDBK (967-5325).

For information about sales to schools and
libraries, call 1-800-975-3250 (United States),
or 1-800-837-5365 (Canada).

Library of Congress Cataloging-in-Publication
Data for this volume has been applied for.

Hello, Beautiful!
ISBN: 978-0-7166-3567-3 (set, hc.)

Colorful Animals
ISBN: 978-0-7166-3569-7 (hc.)

Also available as:
ISBN: 978-0-7166-3579-6 (e-book)

Printed in China by Shenzhen Wing King Tong
Paper Products Co., Ltd., Shenzhen, Guangdong
1st printing July 2018

Staff

Writer: Shawn Brennan

Executive Committee

President
Jim O'Rourke

Vice President and
Editor in Chief
Paul A. Kobasa

Vice President, Finance
Donald D. Keller

Vice President, Marketing
Jean Lin

Vice President,
International Sales
Maksim Rutenberg

Vice President, Technology
Jason Dole

Director, Human Resources
Bev Ecker

Editorial

Director, New Print
Tom Evans

Managing Editor, New Print
Jeff De La Rosa

Senior Editor, New Print
Shawn Brennan

Editor, New Print
Grace Guibert

Librarian
S. Thomas Richardson

Manager, Contracts &
Compliance (Rights &
Permissions)
Loranne K. Shields

Manager, Indexing Services
David Pofelski

Digital

Director, Digital Content
Development
Emily Kline

Director, Digital Product
Development
Erika Meller

Manager, Digital Products
Jonathan Wills

Graphics and Design

Senior Art Director
Tom Evans

Senior Visual
Communications Designer
Melanie Bender

Media Researcher
Rosalia Bledsoe

Manufacturing/
Production

Manufacturing Manager
Anne Fritzinger

Proofreader
Nathalie Strassheim

Contents

Introduction

Welcome to "Hello, Beautiful!" picture books!

This book is about colorful animals. Each book in the "Hello, Beautiful!" series uses large, colorful photographs and a few words to describe our world to children who are not yet reading on their own or are beginning to learn to read. For the benefit of both grown-up and child readers, a picture key is included in the back of the volume to describe each photograph and specific type of animal in more detail.

"Hello, Beautiful!" books can help pre-readers and starting readers get into the habit of having fun with books and learning from them, too. With pre-readers, a grown-up reader (parent, grandparent, librarian, teacher, older brother or sister) can point to the words on each page as he or she speaks them aloud to help the listening child associate the concept of text with the object or idea it describes.

Large, colorful photographs give pre-readers plenty to see while they listen to the reader. If no reader is available, pre-readers can "read" on their own, turning the pages of the book and speaking their own stories about what they see. For new readers, the photographs provide visual hints about the words on the page. Often, these words describe the specific type of animal shown. This animal may not be representative of all species, or types, of that animal.

This book displays some of the many kinds of colorful animals that live throughout the world. Help inspire respect and care for these important and beautiful animals by sharing this "Hello, Beautiful!" book with a child soon.

Chameleon

Hello, beautiful chameleon!

You are a panther chameleon. You are a type of lizard that can change your color!

You use your long, sticky
tongue to catch a bug to eat.

Duck

Hello, beautiful duck!

You are a mandarin duck.
You live on or near water.

You are covered in feathers of bright purple, green, brown, and white.

Fish

Hello, beautiful fish!

You are a longnose hawkfish. You live in a colorful, rocky part of the ocean.

You have a long nose! There are **red** and white lines across your body.

Frog

Hello, beautiful frog!

You are a **blue** poison dart frog. You are a slimy animal that lives in water and on land.

You have skin that will hurt us if we touch you! Your bright color warns us to stay away!

Lizard

Hello, beautiful lizard!

Your are an eastern collared lizard. You are blue and yellow with black rings around your neck.

Your body is covered by little pieces called scales.

You can run fast
on your hind legs!

Monkey

Hello, beautiful monkey!

You are a mandrill. You live in forests.

You are big. You have bright blue cheeks and a flat red nose.

Moth

Hello, beautiful moth!

You are an elephant hawk moth.
Your body and
wings are
pink.

You looked like a tiny elephant's trunk before you grew into a moth!

Octopus

Hello, beautiful octopus!

You are a **blue-ringed** octopus. You have big eyes and eight long arms.

Your bite can hurt us!

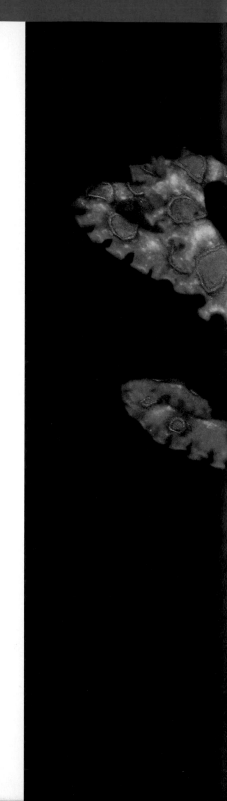

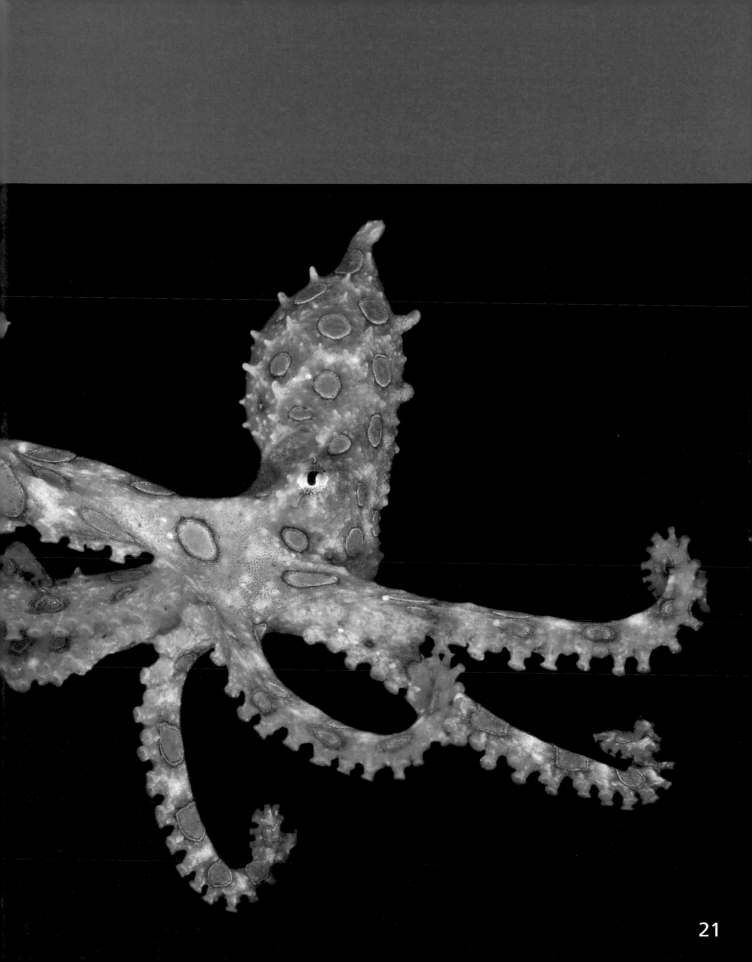

Parrot

Hello, beautiful parrot!

You are a scarlet macaw.
You live in warm forests.

You are a parrot with
a long tail and blue,
red, yellow, and
green feathers.

You fly high in the jungle. You are noisy!

Snake

Hello, beautiful snake!

You are a rainbow boa.
You have a long body and
no legs.

You are a reddish-brown
snake. But in sunlight you
shine with the colors of
the rainbow.

Spider

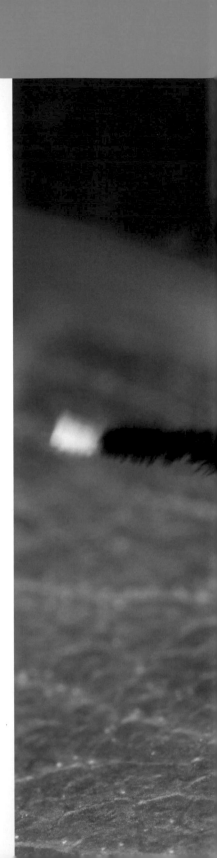

Hello, beautiful spider!

You are a peacock spider. You have eight legs.

You like to dance and show your pretty colors!

Wasp

Hello,
beautiful wasp!

You are a cuckoo
wasp. You are a
small flying animal.

You are colored like a rainbow!

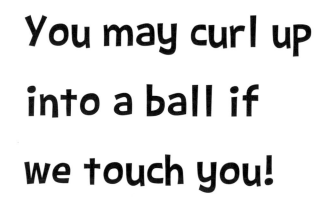

You may curl up
into a ball if
we touch you!

Picture Key

Learn more about these colorful animals! Use the picture keys below to learn where each animal lives, how big it grows, and its favorite foods!

Chameleon

Hello, beautiful chameleon!

You are a panther chameleon. You are a type of lizard that can change your color!

You use your long, sticky tongue to catch a bug to eat.

Duck

Hello, beautiful duck!

You are a mandarin duck. You live on or near water.

You are covered in feathers of bright purple, green, brown, and white.

Fish

Hello, beautiful fish!

You are a longnose hawkfish. You live in a colorful, rocky part of the ocean.

You have a long nose! There are red and white lines across your body.

Pages 6-7 Chameleon

The panther chameleon *(kuh MEE lee uhn)* lives in the forests of Madagascar, an island off the east coast of Africa. Males grow to 12 to 18 inches (30 to 45 centimeters). Females are much smaller. The panther chameleon primarily eats insects and other small creatures.

Pages 8-9 Duck

The mandarin duck lives in China and Japan. It is 16 to 19 inches (41 to 49 centimeters) long with a 26- to 30-inch (65- to 75-centimeter) wingspread. It eats mainly plants and seeds, but it will also eat snails, insects, and small fish.

Pages 10-11 Fish

The longnose hawkfish lives in tropical reefs in the Indian and Pacific oceans. It grows to about 5 inches (13 centimeters) long. It mainly eats tiny marine *invertebrates* (animals without backbones).

Frog

Hello, beautiful frog!

You are a blue poison dart frog. You are a slimy animal that lives in water and on land.

You have skin that will hurt us if we touch you! Your bright color warns us to stay away!

Lizard

Hello, beautiful lizard!

Your are an eastern collared lizard. You are blue and yellow with black rings around your neck.

Your body is covered by little pieces called scales.

You can run fast on your hind legs!

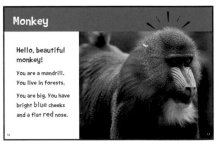

Monkey

Hello, beautiful monkey!

You are a mandrill. You live in forests.

You are big. You have bright blue cheeks and a flat red nose.

Pages 12-13 Frog

The blue poison dart frog lives in the southern part of the South American country of Suriname. Adult blue poison dart frogs range from 1 1/4 inches to 1 3/4 inches (3 to 4.5 centimeters) in length. They mainly eat ants, mites, and termites. They also eat beetles and millipedes. The skin of this frog is toxic to the touch.

Pages 14-15 Lizard

The eastern collared lizard is also called the common collared lizard. It is chiefly found in dry, open regions of the southwestern United States and in Mexico. It reaches 8 to 14 inches (20 to 36 centimeters) in length, including the tail. Eastern collared lizards eat grasshoppers, crickets, and other insects. They also eat other small animals, including lizards.

Pages 16-17 Monkey

The mandrill *(MAN druhl)* lives in the forests of the country of Cameroon and other parts of western Africa. Male mandrills are among the largest monkeys, weighing as much as 90 pounds (41 kilograms). Female mandrills weigh half as much. They feed on vegetation—especially fruits—and many kinds of insects.

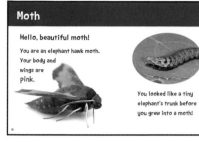

Moth

Hello, beautiful moth!

You are an elephant hawk moth. Your body and wings are pink.

You looked like a tiny elephant's trunk before you grew into a moth!

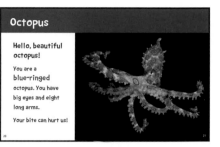

Octopus

Hello, beautiful octopus!

You are a blue-ringed octopus. You have big eyes and eight long arms.

Your bite can hurt us!

Parrot

Hello, beautiful parrot!

You are a scarlet macaw. You live in warm forests.

You are a parrot with a long tail and blue, red, yellow, and green feathers.

You fly high in the jungle. You are noisy!

Pages 18-19 Moth

The elephant hawk moth lives across much of Europe and Asia. It is a common moth in the United Kingdom and Ireland and has been introduced into British Columbia in Canada. It has a wingspread of 2 to 3 inches (5 to 7 centimeters). It feeds on the nectar of honeysuckle and other tubular flowers.

Pages 20-21 Octopus

The blue-ringed octopus is commonly found along the southern Australian coast. Its body is about the size of a golf ball. They mainly eat small crabs and shrimp, but they will also feed on any fish they can catch. The bite of this octopus can kill a person.

Pages 22-23 Parrot

The scarlet macaw *(muh KAW)* lives in forested areas of South America, Central America, and Mexico. They grow to more than 30 inches (75 centimeters) in length, up to half of which is the long tail feathers. They mainly eat nuts, seeds, and fruit.

Snake

Hello, beautiful snake!

You are a rainbow boa. You have a long body and no legs.

You are a reddish-brown snake. But in sunlight you shine with the colors of the rainbow.

Spider

Hello, beautiful spider!

You are a peacock spider. You have eight legs.

You like to dance and show your pretty colors!

Wasp

Hello, beautiful wasp!

You are a cuckoo wasp. You are a small flying animal.

You are colored like a rainbow!

You may curl up into a ball if we touch you!

Pages 24-25 Snake

The rainbow boa lives in South America and lower Central America. Adults reach an average length of 5 to 6 feet (1.5 to 1.8 meters). They eat rodents, lizards, birds, and other small animals.

Pages 26-27 Spider

The peacock spider lives in parts of Australia. They are less than $1/4$ inch (6 millimeters) in body length. They eat insects, killing prey several times their size. A female peacock spider will sometimes eat the male if she is not impressed by his dancing!

Pages 28-29 Wasp

Cuckoo wasps live everywhere except Antarctica. Most are smaller than about $1/2$ inch (1.2 centimeters) in length. Cuckoo wasps sneak their eggs into the nests of other insects. The young hatch and feed on the eggs and *larvae* (young) there.

Index